Young
Eleanor
Roosevelt

Young Eleanor Roosevelt

by Francene Sabin
illustrated by Marcy Dunn Ramsey

Troll Associates

Library of Congress Cataloging-in-Publication Data

Sabin, Francene.
  Young Eleanor Roosevelt / by Francene Sabin; illustrated by Marcy
Dunn Ramsey.
    p.   cm.
  Summary: Recounts the early life of the first lady and
humanitarian who grew up with ''Uncle Teddy'' Roosevelt and found an
outlet for her intelligence and energy by working in resettlement
houses.
  ISBN 0-8167-1779-6 (lib. bdg.)   ISBN 0-8167-1780-X (pbk.)
  1. Roosevelt, Eleanor, 1884-1962—Childhood and youth—Juvenile
literature.   2. Presidents—United States—Wives—Biography—
Juvenile literature. [1. Roosevelt, Eleanor, 1884-1962—Childhood
and youth.   2. First ladies.] I. Ramsey, Marcy Dunn, ill.
II. Title.
E807.1.R48S23   1990
973.917'092—dc20
[B]
[92]   89-33939

Printed in the United States of America.
10 9 8 7 6 5 4 3

Young Eleanor Roosevelt

"H-E-L-P! H-E-L-P!"

The cries and screams swirled around young Eleanor Roosevelt as she stood on the deck of the *Britannic*. Terror spread quickly after the large ocean liner had been accidentally rammed by another ship. The *Britannic* had left New York for Europe only a day ago. Now, it was in danger of sinking.

Eleanor was just two and a half years old. She watched in horror as people scrambled for the safety of the lifeboats waiting below. Many passengers were hurt—some in the collision, others in the crush of people panicking. Nearly everyone was now pressed against the railing of the ship. They were waiting their turns to climb down the rope ladders into the lifeboats.

Eleanor was too small to climb down into a lifeboat. So one of the sailors lifted her up. He was going to drop her into the arms of her father, Elliott, who was in a lifeboat directly under them. But Eleanor was terrified by all the screaming, shouting, and especially by the tossing of the flimsy lifeboats on the waves.

Papa seemed to be miles away. Eleanor clutched the sailor's neck and sobbed with fear. But he pulled her hands free and dropped her the long distance to her waiting father. Eleanor was relieved to be safe again in her father's arms. But her heart was still pounding with terror.

The Roosevelts returned to New York, then
began preparing to sail again for Europe. Eleanor
was still so scared that she begged her parents
to stay home. But they were determined to go.
Eleanor was left behind with her father's aunt,
Anna Gracie.

As sweet and kind as Mrs. Gracie was, she was
not Eleanor's mother or father. Eleanor felt that
her parents had gone away to punish her for being
such a bad girl on the damaged ship. She was sure
she had disgraced them by showing so much fear.
All through her life, Eleanor Roosevelt felt she
had to prove that she had courage.

10

Almost from the day she was born—October 11, 1884—Anna Eleanor Roosevelt was called Eleanor. She was a beautiful baby, with big blue eyes and pale blonde hair. Her birth was announced in all the New York newspapers. But that wasn't surprising. Nearly every event in the Roosevelt family's life was of interest to the public. Eleanor's father, Elliott, was a very rich man. He was also a brother of Theodore Roosevelt, who would become the twenty-sixth President of the United States.

Anna Hall Roosevelt, Eleanor's mother, was a member of a very important American family too. Three of her ancestors had signed the Declaration of Independence. Anna was beautiful and popular in society. She and Elliott Roosevelt were considered a golden couple.

Elliott Roosevelt adored his little girl. He called her "Golden Hair" and "Little Nell." As soon as she could walk, Eleanor toddled into her father's room early every morning. He welcomed her with hugs and kisses. Then, while he got ready for the day, she chattered and danced around the room. Eleanor later remembered "twirling round and round until he would pick me up, throw me into the air, and tell me I made him dizzy."

But there weren't enough of those wonderful mornings with her father. Elliott Roosevelt was often away from home. Sometimes he traveled on business. Other times he was in a hospital because of illness.

The Roosevelts were part of a large family who were always doing things. They visited each other quite often—for Sunday dinners, holidays, birthday parties, and summer weekends.

When Eleanor was two years old, one of these visits was to the home of James Roosevelt, in Hyde Park, New York. James Roosevelt was a distant cousin of Eleanor's father. His son, Franklin, who was four years old, was Elliott Roosevelt's godson. After the whole family had dinner, the children were sent to the nursery to play. "I am told that Franklin, probably under protest, crawled around the nursery with me on his back," Eleanor Roosevelt wrote many years later.

They were just two little children playing. Nobody could have predicted their memorable future together. Franklin Delano Roosevelt would grow up to become the thirty-second President of the United States and the only U.S. President ever to be elected to that office four times. Eleanor Roosevelt, his wife through all those years, would carve a remarkable record of her own in the history of our country.

The relatives whom Eleanor saw most often were Uncle Teddy and Aunt Edith Roosevelt, and their children. Uncle Teddy was an energetic, horse-riding, fun-loving man. When he wasn't doing government work in Washington, D.C., his greatest pleasure was romping with the children—his and everyone else's. Uncle Teddy was Eleanor's favorite relative. He, in turn, loved his little niece very much.

When her father was ill and away from home, Eleanor found plenty of fun and play at Uncle Teddy's estate at Sagamore Hill, Long Island, New York. At home, she had to be very quiet and well-behaved. But at Uncle Teddy's, there were no hard rules to follow. All the children— and there were always lots of them around— were free to do just about anything they wanted.

And Uncle Teddy loved to join in for swimming, sailboating, tree climbing, horseback riding, fishing, and playing games. Sagamore Hill was the one place where Eleanor could really be a child, and she looked forward to every visit to Uncle Teddy's.

In happy times or sad, Eleanor Roosevelt always tried to be useful to others. But she also struggled with the fears many children have. "Looking back," she wrote later, "I see that I was always afraid of something—of the dark, of displeasing people, of failure."

Eleanor's fears and her devotion to helping others finally clashed when she was about thirteen years old. Eleanor was visiting her aunt Edith Hall, who was ill with a sore throat. She liked doing things for her aunt. But one night, Aunt Edith called to her. She asked Eleanor to go to the basement to get some ice from the icebox. But the icebox was three flights of stairs down in the dark. Eleanor would be alone in the basement, with no light, groping her way toward the icebox!

"My knees were trembling," wrote Eleanor.
"But between the fear of going and the fear of
not being allowed to help Aunt Edith when she
was ill, I had no choice. I went and returned
with the ice." Eleanor's fear of the dark was
not as great as the love she had for her aunt.
And throughout her life, Eleanor Roosevelt would
overcome fear out of her stronger desire to aid
others.

Helping others was a Roosevelt family tradition. Eleanor's grandfather, Theodore Roosevelt, after whom Uncle Teddy was named, had helped to set up clubhouses for newsboys. These houses were shelters providing a place to sleep and hot meals.

In those days, there were no government programs to help poor people of any age. Orphan boys often tried to survive by selling newspapers on the street. This kind of work paid almost nothing. Usually, what a newsboy earned was not enough to buy a decent meal. And it was never enough to pay for a warm place to sleep. Newsboys as young as five years old slept in doorways, on park benches, in hallways, or anywhere else they could. Summer was bearable. But during the winter, many of them froze to death.

Theodore Roosevelt was a trustee of the Children's Aid Society. He got together with his friends and paid all the expenses for a number of newsboy clubhouses. The boys paid a penny or two for a meal and a bed. That way, the boys did not feel they were taking charity, but instead were paying their way. Of course, the main expenses and the day-to-day work were taken care of by people like the Roosevelts.

Eleanor was only five when she made her first visit to a clubhouse. It was Thanksgiving Day, 1889, when she and her father brought and served Thanksgiving dinner to a large group of newsboys. On the way there, Eleanor's father explained that this was the real meaning of Thanksgiving. The Roosevelts were fortunate to have so much. It would be wrong, he said, for them not to share with others. After all, how could they consider themselves good people if they knew others were suffering and they did nothing to help?

The newsboy clubhouses were not the only forms of public service Eleanor was expected to help with. Grandfather Theodore had also established a hospital for children. There, children with broken bones or crippling conditions were brought for treatment. Most of the patients could not afford medical care. The hospital depended on people like the Roosevelts to pay expenses and act as volunteers.

The family of Eleanor's mother, the Halls, were just as involved in charitable work. Grandmother Hall took Eleanor to the children's ward at the Post-Graduate Hospital every Christmas. They brought Christmas trees, decorations, and gifts for the young patients. The Halls also took Eleanor to settlement houses, where they did volunteer work.

A settlement house was a community center in poor neighborhoods. People could go there for help. The settlement houses had doctors, nurses, teachers, clergy, cooking instructors, and other volunteers. Many immigrant families found encouragement and guidance at their local settlement house.

From her very first visit, Eleanor had great satisfaction working at a settlement house. It gave her a way to be useful. It was also an outlet for her intelligence and energy.

From childhood on, Eleanor Roosevelt wanted to do good and make people happy. When her brother Elliott was born in 1889, Eleanor helped take care of him. She wanted to make her mother smile. And she also wanted to make her father well. But her parents' problems were more than a little girl could solve.

In 1890, Eleanor, her baby brother Elliott, and her parents went to Europe. It was hoped that a long, trouble-free vacation would make Mr. Roosevelt well again. For a while it worked, and the family was enjoying the trip. Then Mr. Roosevelt became sick again, and he had to enter a hospital in France.

Mrs. Roosevelt rented a little house in Paris. Every day, she visited her husband at the hospital. It worried her that she did not have enough time to be with Eleanor and Elliott, Jr. She was also expecting another baby, and she needed to rest.

Until now, Mrs. Roosevelt had taken care of her daughter's education. But that wasn't possible anymore. Then a friend suggested that Eleanor be put in a nearby convent school. Mrs. Roosevelt thought this was a fine idea. It was also a fine opportunity for Eleanor to learn French. Most of all, she would be well cared for, day and night.

Six-year-old Eleanor was very unhappy at the school. All the other girls were French. They spoke so quickly that Eleanor could not understand what they were saying. She felt left out and unliked, and she missed her family. Eleanor worried that something could happen to one of them and she would never know.

Then, one day, a schoolmate of Eleanor's swallowed a coin by accident. The girl drew a lot of attention, and this gave Eleanor an idea. Eleanor said that she had also swallowed a coin. But it was obvious to the teachers that her story was not true. The headmistress knew that Eleanor was doing this to get attention. "You will not be punished," the headmistress told her, "if you will just tell the truth. And then all of this will be forgotten."

Eleanor was ashamed of her lie, but she was too embarrassed to confess. Finally, the headmistress sent for Mrs. Roosevelt and asked her to take Eleanor out of the school. Eleanor was crushed. She felt she had disgraced her family. But Eleanor took comfort from being back again with her mother and her brother Elliott. Best of all, Mrs. Roosevelt was going to take the children home to America.

Soon after they returned, Mrs. Roosevelt gave birth to another boy, who was named Hall. Eleanor was thrilled to help take care of her new baby brother. She rocked his cradle, ran errands for the nurse, and even took charge of young Elliott. Eleanor also rubbed her mother's forehead. Mrs. Roosevelt had bad headaches, and she often said that Eleanor's soft hands were the best treatment she knew of.

Mr. Roosevelt then returned to the United States. But he could not stay with the family in New York. The climate was not good for his health. So he went to live with cousins in the Virginia countryside. Eleanor hoped her father would get well enough to come home. But he never did.

When his health permitted, Elliott Roosevelt came home for brief visits. These were Eleanor's happiest moments. Papa took "Little Nell" out driving in his carriage, to the ballet, to the theater, and to other places she enjoyed. In between those wonderful visits, she felt her father's love and care through his letters. Eleanor Roosevelt saved every letter her father had ever sent her.

Mr. Roosevelt also looked forward to the day when he would be able to come home. In his letters to his daughter, he often talked of it. When Eleanor celebrated her eighth birthday, she received this message from her father: "Many happy returns on this birthday, Little Nell. I am thinking of you always, and I wish for my girl the greatest of joy and the most perfect happiness in her sweet young life.

"Because Father is not with you is not because he doesn't love you. For I love you tenderly and dearly. And maybe soon I'll come back all well and strong, and we will have such good times together as we used to have."

Papa's letters and the hope for a happy future kept Eleanor's spirits strong even in the worst of times. One such time came in December 1892 when her mother died of diphtheria. Today, people in the United States are vaccinated against diphtheria at a very young age. But in the late nineteenth century, that wasn't true. And so the disease took many lives.

After Eleanor's mother died, the children went to live with Grandmother Hall. Then, in the spring of 1893, another tragedy struck the family. Four-year-old Elliott, Jr., died from the same disease that claimed his mother—diphtheria. Mr. Roosevelt tried to console his daughter through his letters. And even though he wasn't actually there with her, Eleanor felt and relied on his strength.

As an adult, Eleanor wrote, "He suggested that I go out and watch a house being built of bricks. He called the bricks good habits, cleanliness, truth, thought of others, self-control, and generosity. He went on to say the mortar is constant repetition, which binds these habits to us. The masons are parents and teachers, guiding and helping. And the finished house is your finished character that—if well built—will be ready to stand rain or shine, good fortune or ill fortune."

In August 1894, Elliott Roosevelt died in a hospital. Within a two-year period, Eleanor suffered the loss of her mother, her brother Elliott, and now her father. She was greatly shaken by all three deaths. Not yet ten years old, Eleanor Roosevelt suddenly became an orphan.

Grandmother Hall took young Eleanor and her baby brother Hall in and did her best to raise them. She saw to it that Eleanor had lessons in music, French, German, dancing, riding, and art. Still, Eleanor was lonely. She wished she could go to school with other children her age. But Grandmother Hall didn't believe in sending girls to school. Instead, she sent Hall away to a boys' school in Massachusetts. Whenever Eleanor visited him there, she thought it was the most wonderful place in the world. Eleanor wished she could go to a girls' school just like it.

That wish finally came true when Eleanor was fifteen years old. Her father's sister, Aunt Bye, saw how sad and lonely she was. So Aunt Bye convinced Mrs. Hall to send Eleanor to a school in England. The school was Allenswood, not far from London. Aunt Bye had attended the school when she was Eleanor's age. She promised Mrs. Hall that Eleanor would become a polished, fine young lady at Allenswood. And so Eleanor sailed for England in the fall of 1899.

The three years Eleanor spent at Allenswood were wonderful. She bloomed as a student, reading every book assigned to her and many more books besides. At Allenswood, Eleanor discovered she had an excellent memory. She could memorize poems after one reading and remember complete sections of books. Eleanor also learned how to ask questions and how to put together ideas.

These skills served Eleanor Roosevelt throughout her life. She wrote many books before she died at the age of 78. One of them, *It's Up to the Women,* published in 1933, encouraged women to do an equal share of the work necessary to bring America out of the Great Depression in the 1930's.

In 1902, Eleanor returned to New York from Allenswood. She was eighteen years old then. Like other girls her age and from her background, Eleanor began going to parties, dances, and other social events. But she also wanted to go to college. Grandmother Hall, however, forbade it. She said that nice young ladies did not go to college. Instead, they made their entrance into fine society and then got married. For energetic Eleanor, that kind of life wasn't enough. And so she devoted her days to working at the Rivington Street Settlement House.

Certainly, there was a pressing need for help such as Eleanor's. In 1902, most of the settlement houses in New York were at the bursting point. Thousands upon thousands of poor European immigrants had come to America. A large number of them stayed in New York, where they flocked to the settlement houses for assistance. Jobs were hard to find. And those immigrants who found one usually worked very long hours for very little pay. Few complained. To complain was to risk getting fired and replaced.

At the settlement house, Eleanor became aware of the miserable, poverty-ridden lives led by the immigrants. She also became aware of the political corruption that allowed these conditions to exist. She realized that helping individual people was doing good, but it wasn't solving society's problems. The solutions included better education, laws to protect workers and the buying public, and better enforcement of the laws already in existence. She spent the rest of her life working toward these ends. And as first lady, Eleanor Roosevelt was a strong force for social change.

The year 1902 was important to Eleanor in another way. Soon after her return to America from England, she met her cousin Franklin again. They enjoyed being together, and they soon fell in love. On March 17, 1905, they were married. The wedding of Eleanor and Franklin Roosevelt was a national event. The bride was escorted to the altar by her uncle, President Theodore Roosevelt.

The marriage was the beginning of a long and productive relationship. Franklin Delano Roosevelt became a President of distinction. Likewise, Eleanor Roosevelt became one of our country's finest first ladies. She was an inspiration to women everywhere.

For many years, Eleanor Roosevelt wrote a daily newspaper column called "My Day." It influenced millions of Americans throughout the country. She spoke out against social injustice, and she spoke for civil rights and for national unity during World War Two.

Eleanor Roosevelt's mental abilities and dedication to doing good combined to make her an ideal choice as United States representative to the United Nations. And it was at the United Nations that she spent some of her most productive years.

Eleanor Roosevelt died on November 7, 1962. She was buried beside her beloved Franklin in the rose garden of their home at Hyde Park, New York. Her death was mourned across America and in many other countries. She had earned the respect and admiration of millions. How proud her father would have been of his "Little Nell"!